Grief

The Universal Emotion Of Loss

by Karla Kay

BALBOA.
PRESS
A DIVISION OF HAY HOUSE

Balboa Press books may be ordered through booksellers or by contacting:

Balboa Press
A Division of Hay House
1663 Liberty Drive
Bloomington, IN 47403
www.balboapress.com
1-(877) 407-4847

ISBN: 978-1-4525-4218-8 (sc)
ISBN: 978-1-4525-4220-1 (hc)
ISBN: 978-1-4525-4219-5 (e)

Library of Congress Control Number: 2011961619

Because of the dynamic nature of the Internet, any web addresses or
links contained in this book may have changed since publication and
may no longer be valid. The views expressed in this work are solely those
of the author and do not necessarily reflect the views of the publisher,
and the publisher hereby disclaims any responsibility for them.

The author of this book does not dispense medical advice or prescribe
the use of any technique as a form of treatment for physical, emotional,
or medical problems without the advice of a physician, either directly
or indirectly. The intent of the author is only to offer information
of a general nature to help you in your quest for emotional and
spiritual well-being. In the event you use any of the information in
this book for yourself, which is your constitutional right, the author
and the publisher assume no responsibility for your actions.

Certain stock imagery © Thinkstock.
Any people depicted in stock imagery provided by Thinkstock are
models, and such images are being used for illustrative purposes only.

Printed in the United States of America

Balboa Press rev. date: 1/12/2012

Dedicated to:

Brent, Lindsey and Tawnee –
Thank you for giving me signs along the way.

To all those who have lost a loved one.

In Appreciation for:

My daughter Bridget for her courage, love,
strength and commitment to life.

My family for your compassion, love,
support and understanding.

My friends for your unwavering friendship.

John, who found a way to open my heart,
for believing in me
and for his dedication to this book.

With Gratitude to:

Those who work in Hospice for the
compassion you bring to families and
patients at the end of life.

Donor Network Society for the heart felt work you
do and the families who donate life to others when
death and grief has entered your world.

Contents

Introduction

In some way I have always felt like I was surrounded by death. Perhaps it began for me with my mother losing her little brother to malnutrition in the Great Depression or when she was widowed at the young age of thirty-two. Possibly it began as an unborn child when my mother had thoughts of suicide. I remember when I was a little girl my parents taking in my great Aunt Ruby and my grandmother to care for them in their last days, they both died in our home, and I recall going to a mortuary as a child and playing with toys as my mother set my great Aunt Ruby's hair.

In 1993 my brother-in-law was suddenly killed on his motorcycle while riding home from work on his birthday and with this sudden death I watched a very close family of four brothers scatter and become disconnected; I stood by as my husband became angry and distant. In 1994 my husband and I along with our two girls, moved from California to Arizona to try to escape the pain of his brother's death, the loss of his job, our home, and my miscarriage. In 1997, I watched my grandmother take her last breath in hospice and twelve hours later I received a call that my niece had died in a car accident. In March of 2003 I stood by as my sister gave birth to her stillborn little girl.

Even with this seemingly recurring theme of the tragedy of death in my life, I have always felt a compassion for those in grief. I began working as a CNA with Hospice in 1994 and then found my way to greater service as a Unit Manager in a hospice in-patient unit. I always sensed a deeper meaningfulness from this work and felt privileged to be at the bedside of hundreds of people who took their last breath in this life. This was the start of my Spiritual Journey as I began to question life.

This book is not an academic or intellectual discussion on the theories of grief and there is no intention to undermine or disrespect the opinions of professionals or experts in the field of grief. This book is written for the person whose life has been changed forever by grief and to offer a bigger picture and greater awareness to the incredible emotional tragedy that accompanies the experience of loss in life.

Grief is an individual experience that transcends age, gender, ethnicity, culture, belief, non-belief, religion, tradition and values. Yet, for most of us who are in the depths of grief, we cocoon ourselves in our suffering and put on a mask so that we appear to others as if we have it all together. No matter how we look at it, grief is a matter of the heart. It is a universal emotion that we all share, yet we still find ways to stuff these emotions and for many of us our pain turns to anger that we project towards others.

In August of 2003 my husband (childhood sweetheart), myself and our two daughters along with two of their friends, were returning home to Phoenix from a California family vacation. I heard a loud noise and I instantly knew our tire had blown out. As hard as I tried to keep control of our Ford Expedition it flipped into a vicious roll over. The next thing I remember was going through a dark tunnel and then immediately I was in a bright light, this light was warm, as if the sun was shining through me. I had never in my life felt so at peace. In front of me were my husband and youngest daughter who were in white and they were telling me it was not my time, I had to go back. As much as I pleaded to stay with them they told me I had to return.

Suddenly I was going through a dark tunnel and the next thing I remember, I heard a terrifying scream from my oldest daughter Bridget "Mommy, mommy please help me!" I found myself in an upside down vehicle, my husband's limp body leaning over in his seat. "Brent, please wake up and help us," I screamed as I tried to wake him up. I got my daughter

Bridget out of her seat belt, and helped my youngest daughter's friend out of the vehicle. I looked over at my baby girl Lindsey (age 11) whose neck was leaning halfway out the shattered window, she was not moving.

There were people everywhere at the scene of the accident who tried to help us; I wouldn't allow anyone to help me until they confirmed my worst nightmare; that my husband, daughter, and Bridget's best friend had died. I was air lifted to the nearest hospital where I was given a fifty percent chance of surviving; I had severe injuries and had lost a lot of blood. As the emergency room doctor wheeled my daughter and me side by side on our gurneys I told her "I'm going to be ok, I love you, and I'll see you soon." After several days in the hospital and months of physical therapy, I realized I had to pick up the pieces of my shattered life. Through the months and years that followed, I worked hard to rediscover my self, put the terror behind me and find a new purpose in life.

Six months after the accident I started a non-profit organization to help others who had lost a loved one to sudden death. As I spent thousands of hours trying to help others, I came to the realization that my own healing had to come first. I spent a couple of years in therapy, I did the training of Byron Katie, I received a certification in Life Coaching, I deepened my practice in Bikram yoga and I found love again. It was through opening up my heart again, giving and receiving love, that this book was born.

It was John who encouraged me to write this book. I love to read and enjoy books that help me expand my mind and way of thinking. John and I were in our local book store and I found myself scanning the grief section. I commented to John "why couldn't someone write a truly emotional, accurate, and inspiring book about grief?" He said "Why don't you write that book?" It was shortly after that I began to have dreams of my husband coming to me and telling me to go back to Kauai where we spent our honeymoon to begin my writing. John and I planned a trip to Hawaii and knew the first day, as we walked down to the beach and saw three homemade crosses in the rocks on the beach in front of us, that we were in the perfect time and place to begin writing this book.

Through my experience I know the meaning of being shattered by grief and the emotional devastation it leaves behind. In this book I share with you how grief changes each one of us, the root of our feelings, and the uncontrollable waves that take our breath away. The heartache of grief is not only about losing a loved one from death. We experience grief from war, violence, rape, abandonment, molestation, disease, loss of our jobs and homes, broken relationships, abduction, addiction and the loss of who we really are in this world.

From the vacuum of grief to how loss becomes our ultimate emotional disabler, this journey takes us into a new paradigm of grief. This book brings a new understanding of a grieving world with the promise of a new day, a new you and a glimpse into grief with a compassionate compass.

It is my hearts desire
that you read this book
one sentence,
one paragraph,
one page
or one section at a time.

~ You Are Not Alone ~

Karla

Part One

The Vacuum
of Grief

Grief Transcends Everything

There are no words to meaningfully describe the emptiness and pain that takes us over in the first grasp from the fist of grief. The clinched knots in our stomach, the screaming tears in our heart that no one else can hear, the bottomless, sinking feeling and the endless thought that this must be a bad dream; these are all true experiences of the emotional vacuum of grief. Even in a life not yet touched by grief, we often find ourselves feeling separated or distant in many ways, yet grief transcends all the common ideas and definitions we believed before about wanting to be left alone or withdrawing from others.

The most extreme passage into grief comes with the ultimate loss of a loved one – death. And because death is permanent, we have no way to negotiate, reverse or undo what has happened. We feel abandoned in the void of emotional isolation and separateness. We wander without direction in The Valley of Despair; this is where there is no hope, no sense of purpose, no will to take another breath, no reason to live, and no light. In this endless moment nothing reflects the existence of even our own life force. This is not a bad place. This is not a wrong place. Even when we wish we were anywhere else, what we're left with is the painful truth that right now this is where we are and this is all there is.

Being in the Now (not replaying yesterday and not imagining tomorrow) is allowing yourself to stop and get in touch with your emotions in the present moment. In grief the Now is not always a place of spirituality or inspiration. Sometimes the Now is the last place we want to be and it feels like that's all there is. We find ourselves trapped in a box of recycled endless thoughts that will not stop the torture of the 'what-if's'. Why then, do so many of us do everything we can to avoid our thoughts, deny our emotions and shut down? We keep busy, reach for something to stop the pain, self-medicate, over-eat, drink excessively, stare at the television for hours or get lost on the computer; any outside distraction is better than feeling. We overwork, obsessively clean, take harmful risks and disconnect ourselves from the world. We do whatever we can to find some way to escape from the agony and pain that we can't explain to anyone – even ourselves, all with the intent to be as numb as we can be.

Grief is Unexpected

The force of grief is an emotional state of being that we involuntarily gravitate to. It is in this unpredictable emotional churning that our human frailty surfaces in a way we can not ignore. The differences in our states of being and our moods all relate to how our physical being resonates both physiologically and experientially. These different sensations of our moods all have particular vibrations or wave lengths that run through our bodies and our nervous system. For example, good moods, happiness and being in love have high vibrational wavelengths where as bad moods, anger or depression have low vibrations. Our instinctual human response is to armor ourselves, to go to a lower vibration and close ourselves off. When our entire being is exposed to terror, our life force experiences 'overwhelm'. It is in this process that we shut down in the sudden realization that life as we knew it has forever changed.

The ocean is a wonderful metaphor for the experience of grief. It is the expanse of the water, the sound of the surf crashing down and the stillness of the beach. Life is like the surf moving at its own will – endless waves finding their way onto the shore and the mix of sand and stones moving out from underneath our feet. We never know what the waves are going to do, how powerful they will be, if they'll knock us down or lift us up. Just as in life there are peaceful days and stormy days. There are days we cherish and want to remember and there are the days we want to forget forever.

For some people grief is like a rip current, unexpected, devastating and more forceful than we can imagine. Unlike violent, crashing waves, a rip current goes unnoticed until we are in the force of it. What happens when we find ourselves in a rip current is we thrash around, get disoriented, lose ourselves and end up at the bottom of the ocean – or we relax our body, allow ourselves to feel the force of the current, be aware of our circumstance, hold our breath and eventually float to the surface and exhale to take in a new breath of life.

Although we experience small rip currents in our every day life, a more expressive way to explain the devastation caused by sudden loss or the impact of tragedy is more accurately imagined as a tsunami. A tsunami is a response from the isolated event horizon of an earthquake. In this metaphor the earthquake could be a kidnapping, a car accident, a suicide, a homicide or a bombing. The tsunami is the shocking news of a death notification, or terminal diagnosis that powerfully engulfs our whole being. This is not a cognitive decision one makes when realizing we are spiraling into a shadowy unthinkable place never known before. It is as if everything is closing in and there is a terrible anxiety and smothering agony squeezing out what life we have left within us.

A Natural Human Condition

Grief is also experiencing an involuntary culmination of unresolved emotions. In the course of a single day, overwhelming grief can take us through a storm of emotions. From anguish to pain – to hopelessness – to rage – to sorrow – to even thoughts of self destruction or suicide. When we are in grief, our emotions are painfully raw, unexplainable and devastatingly real.

No two people grieve alike; it is the ultimate individual experience. Our life experience is unique to who we are, how we choose to feel and the thoughts we choose to have. No one experiences loss the same way; this is the one place where judgment or comparison have no access.

It is natural for others not to understand our grief. They can try to sympathize or empathize and they can imagine that they are relating, when in reality others are incapable of understanding our exact experience. People on the fringe of grief feel helpless when they see another suffering because it opens their own suffering. This is why we do not receive any comfort when someone says to us "I know how you feel" because in truth, no one knows exactly how someone else feels. This is where others efforts to 'fix' things leaves us feeling as though there is something wrong with us. What people who have never experienced loss do not fully realize is this is not something anyone can fix. Although grief is an emotional wound that eventually heals over time, grief leaves an indelible scar. When our bodies are injured, over time the wound eventually heals. Yet, even though the wound has healed, the threat of infection is gone and the pain has disappeared, the cells are forever altered and leave us with a scar. This example of the physical healing process is also a perfect metaphor for grief.

Grief Is A Place Not A Time

Grief is not linear. Because each one of us is unique we experience loss differently. There is no standard, no average, for how much time someone 'should' grieve or how long someone 'needs' to grieve. In the eyes of others they may think "you should be over it" after a certain amount of time. A more accurate perspective is that each person takes their own path through grief and time is not a factor.

When others suggest that enough time has passed, it is most often because of their own uneasiness and need for us to get back to the person we were before.

There are some of us who may never make it to acceptance of our loss in a way that seems reasonable to others. This is why it is so important to remember that there is no time period or time limit for grieving. The idea that we can cry and ache for a few days or weeks and then get back to everyday life as usual is an uneducated notion. After the loss of a loved one, there is no such thing as life as usual.

Time is different for each of us. Why is it then that our society makes time so significant in grieving? In grieving each of us find our own way in our own time to heal the wounds in our heart and spirit. For others, who have not experienced grief, they may feel as though at the one year mark there is something 'wrong' with us if we are not back to 'normal'. What many people don't understand is that for now, this is our normal. How can one possibly go back to being the person they once were when the energy of a loved one that filled an irreplaceable space in their life is gone? How can one go back to what was normal after the loss of a marriage, the loss of childhood innocence from violence, the loss of who we were before we were raped or the unimaginable loss of our limbs? The person we once were has changed, whether we wanted change or not.

When we don't push ourselves we begin to realize that every moment has its perfect timing in our lives. We can not force limits on natural human expressions. This is where the place comes in. The place is where we are in each moment of our experience. When we are in this place, we are in what seems to be an eternal twilight. We are between two worlds connecting ourselves to what we once knew and the unknown.

Between Two Worlds

In the vast emptiness of grief, consumed in a silent storm of emotions, we feel disoriented and life becomes meaningless in a world where it seems like there is no day or night. No sense of anything being real or certain. Grief is like having an out of body experience.

Between Two Worlds is the domain of shock. When we are in shock our emotional body shuts down, our physical and mental bodies instinctually respond and take over to manage the traumatic experience. This is why we are able to make funeral arrangements, take care of every day things, call people, or get ourselves out of sudden harm. It is as if we become super human. Grief creates the sensation that life is now a "moment to moment" condition of ultimate inner chaos; it is a congregation of emotions.

When we are between two worlds there is a part of us that becomes angelic-like, as though we are not connected with our bodies, we feel weightless. Our minds seem silenced, aware of the here and now and at the same time not here and now at all. When we come down to earth our emotions surface, creating the pain of our physical bodies and the mental thoughts that begin to torment us. Because we are emotional beings, most of us are good at shutting down our emotions. We spend so much energy focusing on our thoughts that we don't tap into our feelings and by shutting our emotions off we are not in touch with what is happening to us physically, mentally or spiritually.

There is often the feeling of numbness and we cannot begin to imagine any possibility of comfort or focusing our attention on an emotion. The emotional numbness is the body still feeling the effects of the shock that has engulfed our being; again this is not a bad or wrong place to be, it just is. This simultaneous experience of the unpredictable highs from allowing our emotions to release and the unexpected downward freefall into numbness from shutting our emotions down creates the opening for an ongoing internal tug of war. However, the awareness of being Between Two Worlds is a sensation that reminds us we are not stuck; we are becoming open to feeling again. Even if for only brief periods, being Between Two Worlds feels as if we are in an abyss of emotions that has no end. It is the ultimate emotional disabler of being in touch with our physical bodies yet our mind and spirit are in another world.

The loneliness is overwhelming.
Other people see me being so strong.
If they only knew.
How long can I wear this mask?

Part Two

The Ultimate Emotional Disabler

The Quicksand of Loss

Grief is not only about death, Grief is also about loss. There is no escaping the eventuality of some kind of loss. Throughout our life loss can take many forms and show up in countless and unexpected ways. When do we start experiencing loss in our lives? For some of us loss is experienced when we are born. In early childhood we may experience loss through our parents neglect or abandonment, molestation, maybe a best friend moves away or we lose a pet. In adolescence, our loss of innocence shapes how we see the world and is usually a generational shared experience; losing a friend to addiction, a boyfriend or girlfriend, someone we know dies from a car accident, gang violence or war. In adulthood we struggle with loss of a job, the foreclosure of a home, divorce, disease, the empty nest syndrome, terminal and mental illness that can and does affect people of all ages, loss of memory and faculties as we age, personal tragedies or the loss of having someone you love ripped from your life.

Throughout our lives the many shapes of loss can seem devastating and we are not always taught or encouraged to allow ourselves to express our emotions of sorrow. Over time we begin to replicate our learned behavior to shut down our emotions. This emotional blackout obstructs our human need to express and release our emotions. For some of us, we stumble through these experiences and try our hardest to pick ourselves up and somehow find a way to pretend to move on, to move as far as we can in the other direction from the pain. For others our walls come up, we stop trusting and we begin the long and painful process of building our fortress with barriers so thick and high that no one can penetrate them. We forget who we are, we give up on ourselves in the dark hope that someday we will find a way to give up on life itself.

The key ingredient of the Quicksand of Loss is our confused temptation to shut ourselves down as a way to escape the pain. This initial element to shutting ourselves down and closing off from our emotions can be the recipe for disaster throughout our lives that we continue to repeat.

Suffering in Silence

Suffering in silence is a common place where many of us go to hide our emotions. When we are not willing to accept the truth we begin to deny our feelings. We put on a mask without realizing that we have replaced who we really are with the impression of being someone else. The mask may have a smile, look friendly or be outgoing so we appear as if we have it all together. The real person behind the mask may be filled with fear, burning with anger and rage, crying or suffocating in deep sorrow.

This is a place where our heart and soul stare into emptiness. We pretend to be someone other than who we really are in that moment. When we are around others trying to fit in, the lies that we tell ourselves secretly eat away at us. Because our mask becomes second nature we forget its presence and we do not understand why others assume we have moved on or why others are surprised when we spontaneously show our painful emotions. For most of us, when people in grief express any type of emotion we feel uncomfortable because their pain is reflecting the emotions we withhold or deny in ourselves. This suffering becomes a death sentence. We feel we deserve this grief; therefore we must bear the pain. It is through bearing this pain, that we bury ourselves. We think as long as our emotions are out of sight, they will also be out of mind. Yet, our emotions continue to emerge because our emotions live in our body.

Our ego tricks our minds to think that as long as we are suffering in silence, this makes us strong and we believe we appear strong to others. On the other hand, if we expose our genuine emotions we imagine that we would appear weak and we would reveal to others that we are powerless. In reality, showing our authentic selves reveals amazing strength. How we go through grief is a testimony on our life itself.

Comfort in Isolation

At the onset of grief there may be a genuine desire for solitude. When we look within, some of us are able to connect with ourselves in a deeper way. Through this reflection we find inner strength to carry on. It is in this solitude that we find comfort. However, if we allow the solitude to perpetuate and we create separation, we find ourselves not in solitude but in isolation. For many, in this deep sorrow and desire to be left alone, our thoughts can lead to loneliness.

In loneliness we detach ourselves from others, from our deep spiritual beliefs and from ourselves. Our thoughts can lead us to dangerous conclusions, that it would be better if we were with our loved one or loved ones. Thoughts of suicide may become seemingly rational here. We think it makes sense to end our own pain and suffering. And we presume we would also end others pain and suffering if we vanished.

In this isolation we completely separate ourselves from our spiritual identity, our angels or our logical foundations. Our ego believes our thoughts. We become fixed and attach ourselves to a single recycled thought and do not question how this thought makes us feel? In this seclusion we lose ourselves, we forget who we are and the difference we can make in other people's lives. As we continue to allow ourselves to go to this place we perpetuate the cycle of building our impenetrable wall around us. The layers of brick can close our hearts off, never wanting to feel love or be loved ever again.

From Vice President Joe Biden's memoir <u>Promises to Keep</u> about the sudden death of his wife Neilia and their baby daughter Naomi from a car accident shortly after his first election to the Senate in 1992: . . . "Most of all I was numb, but there were moments when the pain cut through like a shard of broken glass. I began to understand how despair led people to just cash it in; how suicide wasn't just an option but a rational option. But I'd look at Beau and Hunter asleep and wonder what new terrors their own dreams held, and wonder who would explain to my sons my being gone, too. And I knew I had no choice but to fight to stay alive."

The Prison of If Only

'Would of, should of, could of, if only' . . . These words can become the dungeon of our thoughts if we allow them to be in the forefront of our minds; endlessly playing and tormenting us with all the possible outcomes that might have been. We imagine there is something we could have done to change what happened, change our fate, change what we said or did in the past or even change the destiny of others. We torture and punish ourselves with the 'if-onlys' in the desperate idea that we can fix everything while we look for someone or something to blame.

The solitary confinement of remorse and regret grinds us into little pieces. Somewhere there is a part of us that knows we cannot go back and change the past, yet we continue to beat ourselves down in this empty relentless cycle of agony and sadness. This is one of the ways we play small in the world – a sure way of keeping us trapped in the quicksand of loss. This is often when and where the pity party takes wing. We strongly believe that if we would have done something different we could have stopped the exact timing of our losses or even of our loved ones death. The 'if-only's' are nothing more than the possible beginnings of depression disguised and gift wrapped in the passion of remorse.

For many of us who have grown up in organized religion, the belief system of being unworthy, undeserving or being a sinner is ingrained into our consciousness. In many religious communities these beliefs can show up in our lives as shame, disgrace, and humiliation. Somehow we find a way to believe that we deserve this punishment that we are putting ourselves through. The truth is that life cannot be controlled and no amount of suffering can change what has occurred in our experience.

As the self imposed desperation of 'if-only's' fill our mind and torture our souls, there must and does come a time to let go of these thoughts. The time to let go is revealed when we allow ourselves to experience the emotions of regret, guilt, and remorse. When we discover there is no way out of the endless recycling of every 'if-only' thought, it is then that we realize we are caught in a loop of painfully unreal beliefs. In this moment we step out of the force of this devastation and into the freedom of surrender.

The Freedom of Surrender

Through it all, there comes a day when we finally say "the hell with it, I'm done with all of this, I want to move forward." This deep realization makes it clear that we cannot change what has happened, yet we can change ourselves and move forward in life. We get to a place of total physical, emotional and mental exhaustion and there are only two choices; one – stay where we are, or two – begin a new life. The first choice isn't really an option. Staying stuck in the dark night of our soul is the same as if we were to sentence ourselves to solitary confinement and life in prison. The second choice is the only genuine option. There is something in each of us, a belief in ourselves, that brings hope into our lives. We long to smile, laugh, and have joy in our life again. Believe it or not, it just happens one day when we decide enough is enough and say to ourselves "I am not going to be like this anymore." We feel like our departed loved ones, our angels – however we relate to them – desire for us to have gratitude for life and to move in a positive direction. It is through living a fulfilling life that we can remain connected with them in a way that honors their memory.

Surrender is not submission, it is not giving up, and it is not about forgetting. True surrender is allowing the possibility of happiness, and aliveness to come back into our life. We are surrendering to a life without agony, guilt, self destruction, anger, blame or fear. We are embracing the moment of inspiration that allows us to let go of our depression, regrets, and endless mental replays of our loss. Throughout our grief, there are layers of letting go that we continue surrendering to. When we completely surrender we are inspired and reconnecting ourselves to the acknowledgment that life is still worth living. Unexpectedly from somewhere deep inside us, the day will come when we find a forgotten strength that motivates us to create a new identity, a new life.

Part Three

The Journey

Bedrock

Few of us ever allow ourselves to go to 'The Rock' – the foundation of our new beginning. Yet, this is a place we must go to before taking the first step on our journey from grief to renewal. For ages it has mystified men and women of religion, philosophers, and poets that only when you feel like you can't go any further, you discover you have hit the bottom and in that instant, transformation begins.

Hitting 'The Rock' is not something we plan or choose to do, we simply find ourselves there with an undeniable knowing sensation. We feel life has been pulled out from underneath us and all our hopes and dreams have come to an end.

Out of this void comes a new dream, a new vision, a new sense of purpose and in the distance a new you.

Transformation has a life force in and of itself that makes its way from unexpected corners of grief and into our souls. This ultimate alone place of absolute desperation and inspiration simultaneously ripples through our entire being. It doesn't matter where we are or what we are doing, suddenly our emotions collide with our thoughts and merge with our spirit into a silent world of near and far, high and low, joy and sorrow. At this still point of self-acceptance, our hearts open and our egos are hushed unveiling a timeless instant of grace.

The First Step

The beginning of the journey in this emotionally intense experience we call grief, often feels like a struggle. After feeling so much emptiness and pain, the idea of another set back or more struggle can bring on a dreadful rush of apprehension. The simple idea that "life could be wonderful again" is wrapped in the doubt and fear that the effort may not be worth the gamble.

The journey of moving forward is made with one new step each day. Even as cliché as this sounds, it is not always easy at first. The journey always begins in our own time. The first step could be at the two year, the fifth year or perhaps even the ten year mark. The key is keeping the will and desire for a new life in our hearts and the motivation to move forward daily, even if it is only with a single small step.

There may be times along the journey when we have to acknowledge "We're not having a great day". Our emotions move, our thoughts change all the time and some days might be tougher than others. What's important to remember is that everyone has off days. The emotional danger is when we let an off-day get a hold of us or take us over and we begin to spiral down into a place of uncertainty; a place where the vulnerability of falling into a slump is so risky. The key is to be careful not to let an off-day become an off-week or an off-month or an off-year. Yet, we want to be mindful not to allow those unexpected dark days to emotionally cripple us. It does not mean we are going to fall back into the quicksand of loss or that we are going to find friendship with isolation. Instead, we realize we are having an off-day and that tomorrow will be another day. We keep our focus and our motivation, on our new desires, our new destinations and our personal healing. Forever is only 24 hours long.

The Upside of Resistance

There is a time, when resistance can serve us. It is when we resist the temptation to go back to those old patterns that prevented us from feeling joy, letting our enthusiasm for life slip away or believing that laughing and living with aliveness has left us forever. This type of resistance has a positive place in our lives and helps to keep us moving forward. At times it can feel like there is a battle going on inside of us. A part of us wants to go back to the same choices that we have always made (the easy way out) and another part of us wants to reach out for a new heightened state of awareness. The danger of reverting back to old patterns and replicating our past is that we find ourselves slipping back into isolation and not connecting with others. Although this can be a conflict, this challenge exists within every one. When we begin to see life with a new perspective and choose not to fall back into the same old routine, we have a feeling of elation that lets us acknowledge we have achieved a huge accomplishment for that day.

When we reach this state of elation, we find ourselves in the Now of our true selves. There is no endless spinning of thoughts of the past and there is no fear or hopelessness in the unknown future. What does happen when we allow our thoughts to be in the present and sustain that vibration of elation is the personal reward of self-esteem and the confidence we receive from the upside of resistance. These positive, self-loving, self-healing feelings put courage back into our lives as we continue to move forward in life. One way to keep us moving forward is coming to the awareness that we need help and we give ourselves permission to reach out to someone.

Asking for Help

Why is it that so many of us have such a difficult time asking for help? For some this reluctance can go as far back as being toddlers when we proclaimed, "I can do it myself!" or in school when we felt silly or dumb for asking questions in the classroom. Many of us grew up in a household where we never heard our parents ask for help or that asking for help may have suggested we were deficient or weak. Yet, in the confusion of grief, what an incredible opportunity we can give to someone else when we let them help us in any way they can.

We have several rooted thoughts that are carried throughout our lives for years and eventually these thoughts can turn into belief systems that we unconsciously use in our daily lives. When we believe that if we ask for help it makes us look vulnerable, why not transform that thought into a different, higher vibrational belief? This transformation is where we start to connect mind, body and spirit together. Asking for help creates an atmosphere of empowerment. It communicates to others that, while we may not have the answers, we are willing to find them and look at the possibilities from different perspectives to make things better.

It is important to remember that we are not losing our minds. The unpredictable, unexpected crushing emotions and feelings from nowhere, that we find ourselves suddenly experiencing, are real. That is why it is so important to have a core of support – those one or two people who we know will always be there for us and love us; someone we trust and know we can count on unconditionally to be there with us on our journey.

Doing One Thing

In grief, the force of devastation can put intense doubt into our lives, preventing us from seeing that one simple action could change everything. The greatest misunderstanding about doing something is about how much power there is in making one decision. The decision to drive drunk or hand our keys to the bartender. The decision to stay in bed all day or go to work. The decision to tell the truth or lie, to live or die. It is so important in the grief process to practice asking ourselves: "What are the consequences of this choice?" "What are the risks when I ignore my intuition?"

Whatever the One Thing is, energy is moving forward into the universe that will move someone else to do One Thing. This is not about right or wrong. We have a tendency to do the same thing over and over again; it becomes a pattern or blueprint for how we choose to cope. This routine either keeps us stuck in the past or motivates us to take a step forward. All of us have patterns; we eat our same favorite foods, go to our favorite restaurants, get dressed a certain way, do our hair the same way and even move our bodies the same way. What would happen if we were to get out of bed differently? What if instead of jumping out of bed, we took a few moments to catch up with ourselves? What would happen if instead of lying in bed, we got up and took a shower? What would happen if we ate less? What would happen if we didn't take another drink? What would happen if we didn't answer the phone? All of our choices come down to doing one thing or another. We need to remember that whatever choice we make, there will be an outcome and that outcome not only effects us, it effects others as well.

Risking Life

For people in grief, risking life could be as simple as getting the mail. It could be more complicated, such as going back to work, having lunch with a friend or going to the market. Anything that has to do with living again now seems to be an incredible risk that might trigger uncontrolled anxiety just by thinking about these things. These are all risks we take to find our way back into a world that seems to be going about its own business. Or is it? How do we know the person taking our food order, bagging our groceries or delivering our mail hasn't experienced some tragedy or loss in their own life?

Life is a mysterious thing. Each of us comes across opportunities every day to truly connect with others. Yet, we pass by with an unconscious-automatic see-saw of "Hello-I'm fine-how are you?" What could happen if someone paused, looked into our eyes and sincerely asked us how we were doing—and we told them, honestly, how we were doing. What could happen when the person who takes our lunch order asks "How are you today?" And we reply, "I'm having a really a terrible day, I'm missing my husband who was killed in the war." Even though this can create a flood of anxiety just thinking about it, look at the opportunity we are giving ourselves to express openly how we feel and at the same time giving someone else the opportunity to relate.

Life works with perfect timing and people always come into our lives for a reason. The shared connections may never take place and the people we share our feelings with would not have had the chance to relate their own experience with us had we not overcome our anxiety, gone out into the world and taken a risk in living out loud in the first place.

~ Karla's Journal ~ September10, 2006 ~

As I lie still, I'm trying to connect with the
emotion that I know I'm suppressing.
Is it guilt, sadness, am I depressed?
No! What I'm experiencing is anger.

Part Four

The Patterns of Grief

The Old Paradigm

Many have written on the subject of grief. Elisabeth Kübler-Ross was one of the leading experts and the most well-known in the field, her views have been adopted by most psychologists, psychiatrists and medical professionals today. As much as Elisabeth Kübler-Ross presented about grief, it is important to acknowledge that her research was based in anticipated death. Ross's model was developed from her professional experiences and insights working in Hospice. Her Five Stages of Grief were arrived at by observing the grieving process of the dying. The Ross model has been unconsciously transferred to the living, those relatives and loved ones of the deceased who were struggling with their loss and grieving an anticipated death.

What Ross originally and other experts later maintained, is that these five stages are states that everyone experiences in grief and when you go through all five stages, you learn to incorporate grief in your life, accept it and eventually move on. Although one can and does at some time go through all of these primary stages, we do not go from one stage to the next in a linear process as some have later interpreted this model. Why grief is so hard to understand from an academic perspective is that it is not limited to only stages, this is the old paradigm of grief. The new paradigm, being presented here for the first time, reveals that there are clusters and layers of grief and these clusters and layers can be experienced independently and simultaneously. This does not suggest that the Ross model is incorrect. It is important to remember that the five stages were discovered in relationship to Anticipated Death.

The Five Stages of Grief have been adopted by many professionals in the field of grief as a linear process. With a linear approach there is a concrete beginning and a concrete end to grief – you begin in denial and you move consecutively from one stage to the next. However, deeper knowing tells us we can also go back and forth between these stages of grief. It is important to note that Elisabeth Kübler-Ross and her foundation acknowledged that the model, contrary to common understanding, is not limited to a linear approach. Yet, this acknowledgement from her foundation has not been fully accepted by all mainstream professionals in their practices.

The Ross Five Stages of Grief

Denial   Anger   Bargaining
Depression   Acceptance

Three additional clinical and academic contemporary approaches that are widely acknowledged in the professional field of grief are these of Therese Rando, Mardi Horowitz and Alan D. Wolfelt.

Researcher and Clinical Psychologist Therese Rando Ph.D. (Institute for the Study and Treatment of Loss) also has contributed a stage model. The Rando model is known as the Six R's.

The Rando Six R's

Recognize   React   Recollect/Re-Experience
Relinquish   Readjust   Reinvest

Psychiatrist Mardi Horowitz M.D. (Director of the Center on Stress and Personality at the Langley Porter Psychiatric Institute) separates the grief process into what he also defines as "stages of loss." These stages, considered by Horowitz to be typical in nature, are flexible and their emergence can be different for everyone and not always in the exact order of his model.

Horowitz's Model of Loss/Adaptation

Out-cry   Denial and Intrusion
Working Through   Completion

Dr. Alan D. Wolfelt noted author, educator and Director of the Center for Loss and Life Transition who is well known for his 5 myths of grief has comforted countless numbers of people with an understanding approach.

The Wolfelt Five Myths of Grief

1. Grief and mourning are the same experience.
2. There is a predictable and orderly progression to the experience of grief.
3. It is best to move away from grief and mourning instead of toward it.
4. Tears expressing grief are only a sign of weakness.
5. The goal is to "get over" your grief.

Although all four professionals mentioned above come to grief with integrity, compassion and an intention to help others; the models and approaches come from a predominately pragmatic point of view and in context to the psychology of grief that is limited to the presentation or acting-out of grief. The amazing thing about grief is, within its huge complexity, the psychology of grief approach is focused on healing; how we outwardly express and demonstrate our pain rather than going to the core of the emotional chaos.

The New Paradigm

The New Paradigm presents the awareness that the grieving process is fluid and often elusive. Unlike the Old Paradigm, the new insights in grief reveal that grief is anything but concrete or with a predetermined set of steps. Integral to the human grieving experience is the reality that many emotions can come and go, overlap and become inter-woven.

In the New Paradigm, the process is experienced through Clusters and Layers of grief rather than stages. In grief the reference points change for each of us depending upon our own experience and the context of the event we endured. Within the realm of loss, there is a fine line between an anticipated event or anticipated death and a sudden event or sudden death. This line is unyielding. In anticipated circumstances we often have a period of time to digest and recognize the oncoming inevitability, no matter how painful or agonizing; in sudden events and sudden death we do not. This has a significant effect on what passage we take through grief.

It is important to understand that, whether anticipated or sudden, the loss of a loved one is an overwhelming and a devastating event. The suffering and trauma of loss is not something that can be measured as greater or lesser or compared as harder or easier to bear because of the nature or horror of the event that takes our loved ones from our lives.

Our complex and fragile human being-ness is at the core of our emotional equilibrium and we all react and face the initial vacuum of grief in our own way, with our own intensity of pain and heartache. It is because of our basic human nature that grief is not a simple five stage process. Whatever the circumstances, grief is processed in a multi-emotional altered state of being.

The Seven Clusters of Grief

A closer look at grief in the new paradigm reveals a more complex web of unpredictable emotional clusters. Within the multi-emotional altered state of being in grief are seven interdependent over-lapping clusters. The Seven Clusters of Grief are: Disbelief – Anger – Guilt – Withdrawal – Sadness – Hope and Renewal. Although similar to the five stages, there are dynamic and subtle differences. Compare for yourself by looking at the Old Paradigm pragmatic and psychological approach versus the New Paradigm patterns shown in the charts on the following pages. The distinctions between the old and the new paradigms will be different depending upon if you have personally experienced grief or you have a limited experience of grief. When we examine the New Paradigm we recognize, in the context of grief, that Disbelief is the inability to believe or admit that a tragic event that has disrupted our life has really happened.

Disbelief is where we can feel as though this is all a bad dream and when we wake up it will all be over. Disbelief is a way for our minds to absorb the shock of what we are presently facing.

Anger is the emotion of extreme irritation and belligerence sparked by what we think is a wrong-doing or an injustice outside of our control. Anger can be one of the easiest emotions for people to cling to because it is usually one of the easiest emotions to have. This is an emotion that people can hide behind for years.

Guilt is the emotion of imposing responsibility, blame or remorse (would of, should of, could of) on one's self. Many of us hold ourselves prisoners to guilt, so we have someone to blame, feeling that we should have prevented our loss in some way. We all have guilt in our lives, sometimes it is the little voice (our conscience) reminding us not to exaggerate the truth. When we allow guilt to become a part of who we are, it becomes toxic like an emotional virus living and eating away at us.

Withdrawal is the side-effect of the desire to become invisible, detached from social or emotional involvement of any kind. It is a technique we use to disappear, to become emotionally sedated or numb in an effort to escape from life. What makes withdrawal so dangerous is that in our seclusion we become irrational. We have no common ground with life interaction. Withdrawal only perpetuates our deepest fears and keeps us frozen in a state of disconnection.

Sadness is rooted in heartache, despondence and sorrow that creates a perpetual whirlpool of separation. There can be a great amount of sadness in each of us and it can live deep beneath the outward image of the 'normal' we portray. Sadness is not an emotion that should be underrated, it has its own vast depths and the lowest state of sadness can feel like depression.

Depression requires a professional's opinion to determine if there is a more prolonged emotional dejection than warranted by any objective reason. There is nothing objective in the personal experience of grief. In the traumatic sadness of grief, often medical and psychological professionals assess and diagnose this state of being as depression. The difference here is significant and it is important for those experiencing sadness in grief to know that sadness, however overwhelming, must not be confused with depression or even clinical depression. Sadness, in its most disabling form, is a condition of psychological trauma.

Hope is the uplifting unexplained expectation for a positive fulfilling outcome we believe will come into our lives. Although there are endless similarities, the idea of hope is unique to everyone. It is that unknown feeling inside of us that says we can make it through this, and we hope for a better day tomorrow. When we rely on trusting ourselves with the desire of letting go and accepting the reality of life in the present, there is a confidence we embrace with optimism and sureness for fulfilling our spirit with renewal.

Renewal is the sensation of rebirth or transformation that brings a new desire for reaching out to live a life beyond grief. This shift can take many forms in yearning for change in our own identity and spiritual enlightenment. In this state of being we replenish ourselves with aspirations for a life filled with new meaning and purpose, unrestrained from the hardship of grief.

It is very important to acknowledge that the Clusters and Layers shared here does not mean these are the only attributes in the New Paradigm. You may feel there are other emotions you relate to more. If you find yourself relating to other patterns or emotions, feel free to replace them with what you feel is the best personal fit for you.

The Seven Clusters of Grief

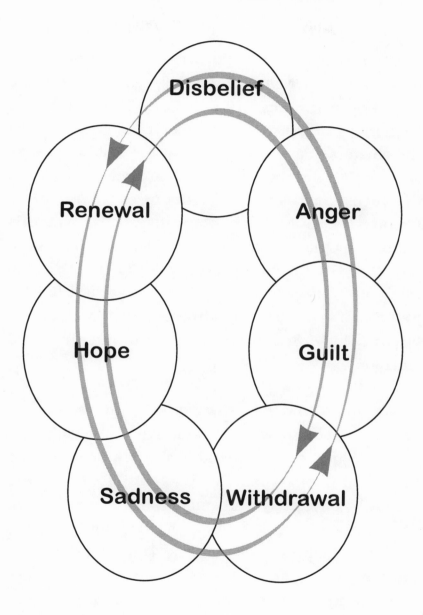

The Eleven Layers of Grief

Huddled around the seven clusters are eleven layers of inter-laced psycho-emotional states of being. Although these layers commonly can manifest one after the other they are not always, in fact rarely, sequential in the way they emerge and collide with the clusters of grief in our life. At times it can feel as though they are coming at us all at once and in other instances it can feel as though one or two haunt us for days on end. As we naturally go through this experience the intensity and confusion of the Eleven Layers of Grief begin to reveal their identities in the form of Overwhelm – Delusion – Rage – Blame – Self-Sabotage – Self-Punishment – Self-Destruction – Despair – Self-Acceptance – Awakening and Harmony.

We now know that when we experience, witness or are given the news of a tragic event, a devastating shock to our system instantaneously puts us into a state of Overwhelm. Every aspect of who we are mentally, physically and emotionally, explodes from the overpowering cognition of the event. In this instant we find ourselves at a loss for relating to anything or anyone – it is as if everything becomes altered and nothing makes sense. Overwhelm takes our breath away and leaves us in an infinite instant, void of everything. What follows is a slow flood of confusion and disorientation that opens the door to Delusion in the shadow of Overwhelm.

The Delusion in grief is unlike the common perception of delusion that professionals apply; it is not the conventional definition of delusion. The conventional perception of delusion is basically that you are crazy; in grief it feels like we are going crazy, however this is the furthest thing from the truth. When people are in the depths of grief, they are experiencing the aftermath of a blazing sensory explosion – the rush of Overwhelm. At its core is Delusion, a confused state we create that is resistant to reason and logic escapes us – the counter-effect and natural involuntary response to being devastated. When coming out of the fog of delusion what we remember as reality hits us with the painful realization of our inability to change, fix, control or undo what happened. This leaves us feeling an intensity of torment, frustration and anger beyond logic that may lead us to Rage.

Rage is that dangerous formula from the emotional eruption of hate, anxiety and violence. Being in a state of full unconscious rage is extremely cruel, so irrational and so malicious that it cannot be contained and the only outlet is to create the role of the victim and lash out at everyone and everything around us. As one begins to exhaust Rage, the need for a reason begins to surface and finding Blame is the most common replacement.

A belief surfaces that you can't exist without finding someone or something to blame and blame manipulates us into becoming the victim. As we blame everyone and everything, we enter a world of endless anguish. There does finally come a time of complete distraught exhaustion, when there is no one person or no single thing left to blame, to judge or despise. At this point there can no longer be a victim. As our suffering intensifies, Blame continues to burn inside us without reason. There must be somewhere to direct justification for our irate Blame, so we turn it on ourselves. We become the Judge and the Victim and having so much hate inside us we cast the verdict of guilty and sentence ourselves. This is when our complicated, self-imposed punishment begins and the layer of Self-Sabotage is peeled back.

Self-Sabotage is that place that has no bottom, no sense of concrete basis. This is where we undermine everything through an effortless skill of procrastination. Being so discouraged we have no will to have or reach any goals or intentions, we create obstacles to assure we are unable to move forward and set into deliberate action the impossibility of living a fulfilled and happy life. This method disables our potential to heal, becoming the signature of Self-Sabotage. At times our Self-Sabotage begins to feel good, like a twisted sensation of accomplishment. We begin to resonate with the lower vibration of hating ourselves and everyone around us and go deeper into our intention to make certain we continue to suffer. When the suffering and rut of Self-Sabotage becomes normal for us, we make it part of our behavior and get no satisfaction in our negative intervention any longer. We may take it one more step lower and enter into the layer of Self-Punishment.

In Self-Punishment we begin to do everything we can to find a host to ease our pain. Going through the layer of Self-Punishment we embrace the feeling that we deserve all of the pain we can endure. We look for anyway we can to condemn ourselves and create as much pain and disconnection as possible. We medicate and abuse ourselves through heavy drinking, over-eating, starving ourselves, becoming addicted to illicit drugs and prescription pain medication, chain smoking or even cutting our own bodies to create physical pain to ease the emotional pain. Again, we eventually come to a level of tolerance, adjusted to the effects of our self-inflicted maltreatment and the suffering we are putting ourselves through loses its impact. We have become comfortably numb. Having no more charge from our chosen method or methods of punishing ourselves, we begin to contemplate other ways of inducing greater pain by harming ourselves or someone else, which can lead to the pinnacle of Self-Punishment – Self-Destruction.

The path of Self-Destruction is the extreme culmination of Rage and a Layer of grief unto itself. It is a condition of absolute torment when the desperate attempt at annihilation (attaining a finality to the suffering) seems to be the only alternative left. This is a place of hollow pitch darkness, where we see no end to the painful chaos of grief and feel nothing more than the emotional war-zone inside us. This is a very dangerous place to be, and in this tortured state of mind the ego is at its peak. We are consumed with only thinking about our self and not of how we destroy the lives of the people around us and those who love us. The strength of acting on this obsessive lower vibrational level can lead to the worst acting-out possible, ending your own life or perhaps taking someone else's.

The true darkness and loneliness of Self-Destruction cannot be foreseen, nor can it be imagined. What is clearly known is that there are only two outcomes from the depths of Self-Destruction. One: The complete and utter tragedy of taking ones own life either slowly or in an instant; and Two:

An unexpected sudden shift into the seemingly bottomless sensation of absolute loneliness. In this spontaneous movement into the void of seclusion, the spirit of our deepest self begins to pulse again and the faintest murmur of light begins to come back to us. This is the first sign we are moving away from Self-Destruction and into Despair.

As odd as it may sound, Despair is the portal to a new beginning. At the onset there is an atmosphere and feeling that there is no hope, ahead is only a dim tunnel of discontent that has no promise to an end of the suffering. Even in the frozen hell of despair, severed from and numb to our own life-force, we still have an instinctive will to exist. At some point and for no clear reason, this invisible will shifts our consciousness from the confinement of Despair to the remembrance of life when it was unbroken. It is in this instant that the feeling of possibility returns, a thought that this is not all there is. We find a way to look beyond and begin to surrender the control of despair to the thought that there is a light ahead, that our life in honoring the memory of our loved ones is worth living. The passage from despair leads us to find peace in the way things are – to reconcile our sorrow and to begin the mourning process. This is an unexpected place of personal healing and empowerment on the threshold to Self-Acceptance.

When we set into motion making amends and reconciling the torment we have put ourselves through, we begin to accept ourselves and love ourselves for living an honest and authentic life. With compassion and love for ourselves, the door opens for not judging or blaming others, this is the first sign of Self-Acceptance. The more one heals through love and acceptance, the more love and compassion there is for others. Accepting ourselves is not always pleasant. Sometimes when we see the hate, anger, blame, selfishness, and self-righteousness in ourselves we are seeing only through our ego. When we become aware of how we are acting and reacting, we can see how we look through the eyes of others and we must acknowledge the painful truth of who we have been and what has happened in our lives.

Another part of Self-Acceptance is acknowledging our good qualities and attributes. When we recognize the greater goodness of our character, we are able to take responsibility for our actions and we begin to forgive ourselves and others. It is through forgiveness that we are able to let go from our thoughts of hate, anger, guilt and blame. We must be aware that forgiveness is a powerful spiritual act and that when we forgive it does not mean that we are condoning or absolving the wrong doing or injustice. What we are doing is releasing the attachment of blame. When we are sincerely able to forgive, we begin to awaken to a new reality with a fresh start and complete Self-Acceptance.

With the possibility of a new reality, we create a foundation for moving forward in life. Through this Awakening there is a meaningful appreciation for how precious life really is. We begin to slow down and become aware of living in the present moment. We realize that through our relationships and connecting with others in our lives, we bring forth sincere gratitude for what we have. Awakening to the possibility of a new you, a new career, a new relationship, or completing something we started before grief consumed our life, is often the first thought we have in moving forward.

The beauty of Awakening lies in understanding that every moment of our life offers us an opportunity to imagine and create a new beginning. When we awaken to our surroundings, we develop a deeper wisdom for living in a conscious world. Through this consciousness we become aware of our words, our actions and how we co-create our life in a world without our loved ones whom we have lost. In the atmosphere of awakening, we gradually accept the idea our departed loved ones, in heart, are always with us and at the same time we are here to fulfill our lives and our destiny. It is in this quiet stillness and peacefulness of awakening that we find our inner compass and begin to balance ourselves with focus on our new direction.

When we work on balancing our lives, the pathway to Harmony is revealed and we realize, ultimately, there is no separation. We understand that we are in a healing process. It is the idea of separation that distracts us and makes us vulnerable to revisiting or succumbing to drifting back to one or more of the other layers or clusters of grief. On a higher level of belief we are at one with our loved ones in every moment of our life. The feeling of being separate from our departed loved ones is only a thought that we create to keep us disconnected – separate from our family, our friends, ourselves and our dreams. There is Harmony in every moment because of the knowing-ness that no matter what comes our way our loved ones in some way are with us. This is a direct link through our mind, body and spirit that connects us to our angelic self.

Eleven Layers of Grief

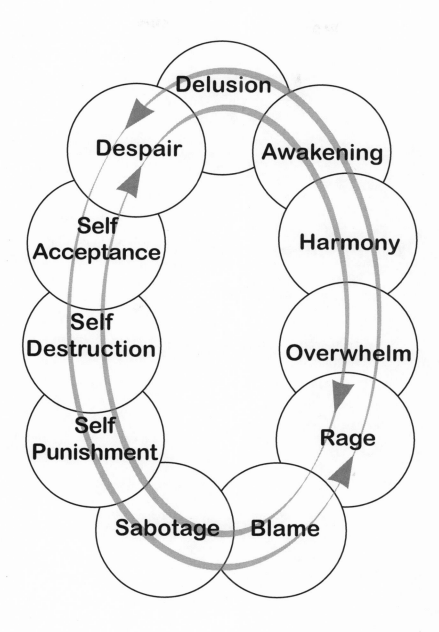

Composite of Clusters and Layers

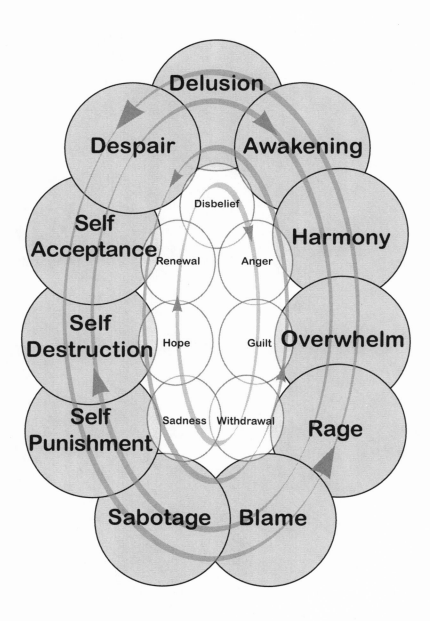

Part Five

The Emotional Anatomy of Grief

The Difference Between Feeling and Emotion

The feeling, thought and emotional collective process are experienced so quickly at times that they can appear to be as one. For many people feelings and emotions are one in the same. A more accurate understanding reveals that there is a great difference from what we are feeling, opposed to our emotions. The awareness of this distinction in every day life is rarely noticed or acknowledged.

The common thought is that feelings and emotions are the same thing with different names, this is not the case. Our feelings are spontaneous and last for less than an instant where as our emotions manifest in our bodies and have physical characteristics.

Our feelings come from a different part of us than our emotions. We could say that our feelings are much more like what we call our intuition. When we have a feeling, there is a heavenly spark of essence that floods our entire being instantaneously. Next, a thought, picture or voice enters our minds. Then an impulse follows and out of the blue we experience a sensation to act on that impulse; all of this happening faster than the speed of light. For example, when we are driving somewhere and suddenly instead of going straight we have a feeling to turn right at the upcoming intersection and we make the unplanned turn, changing our route but still taking us to the same destination – this is a feeling. Another example is when we surprisingly have a feeling to pick up the phone and call a friend or send a friend a message for no particular reason and then discover that the timing was perfect and they were either thinking of us at the same time or at that moment they really needed to talk with someone.

The field of emotions is another world of experience all together. Unlike the intuitive nature of feelings, it is when we attach ourselves to a feeling that it becomes an emotion. Our emotions have stealth like anchors deep inside of us and over time, when not allowed to be released, build up within us. Emotions are recognized by more of a physical sensation and subconscious thought based knowing combined. Our emotions are expressive actions of our conscious state of being in which happiness, sadness, love, hate, confidence, fear, joy, sorrow and others are experienced. Always accompanied with the display of our emotions is some form of physiological sensation or change in our bodies, such as increased heart rate, change in breathing, shaking, crying, laughing, smiling or a full range of other physical symptoms and expressions. Perhaps we begin to realize, for the first time, that experiencing our emotions is our highest form of healing and our most potent method of personalized therapy for moving through every cluster and layer of grief to an acceptance of renewal and wholeness again.

Surrounded by Memories

Our bodies work through cellular, sensory and emotional memory and these human qualities are at the foundation of our grieving process. The emotions of grief are so intense that they transcend our psyche and go far beyond our own personal comprehension. Due to the cellular, sensory, and emotional anchors deep inside of us, these memories may suddenly appear in flashes and can leave us feeling paralyzed and isolated especially when rooted in trauma.

Whether experiencing first-hand, witnessing or receiving unexpected news of a terminal diagnosis or a sudden death, the shock and trauma of an event or experience is so intense that our emotional condition is instantly embedded in our cellular memory. It is in this non-negotiable reflex, that occurs throughout our entire being, that our physical body is actually thrust into overwhelm and every system in our body is altered. This instantaneous reactive dynamic of emotional overload internalizes and ignites the autonomic nervous system and the limbic brain (our emotional brain). Emotionally overwhelming responses to events that take place in our life adhere themselves into our cellular structure – our cellular memory. This is why when we experience seemingly unexpected physical symptoms such as chronic fatigue, breathlessness, tightness in chest, headaches, lower back pain or other ailments; it is possible that our bodies are reacting to our cellular memory being triggered.

Without thought we constantly retain impressions of sensory stimulus even after the stimulus itself has ended or vanished from our experience. Our sensory memory is quietly nesting in the remote undercurrents of our mind created by the things we see, hear, smell, touch and on some occasions taste. The technical terms for the four main forms of sensory memory are: Iconic memory (sight), Echoic memory (hearing), our Olfactory memory (smell), Haptic memory (touch), and subconsciously on the fringe of our basic senses is Gustatory memory (taste), our fifth sense. Although there are sensory registers for all our senses, our most common and predominant senses in crisis are sight, sound and smell. This is why, for example, when we see a horrible car accident, hear screaming or smell smoke we instantly tense up, adrenalin charges through and the memories of our own experience flashes through us. This involuntary experience of being thrust into sudden remembrance or recall awakens our emotional memory.

The emotional memory of grief is where we find ourselves helplessly in a freefall and the emotions we were consumed in at the time of our crisis overtakes us again. We feel the intensity of the anxiety, certain parts of our bodies ache and hurt, our moods shift abruptly and it is as if we are, once again, in that dark corner of life. Sometimes for only a few moments and other times for hours or days we struggle with being cocooned in emotions we have worked so hard to forget rather than release. It is our emotional memory that triggers our clusters and layers. It is our emotional memory that is held and locked in our bodies, that makes us so vulnerable to finding ourselves again in the quicksand of loss.

Holding on to our Emotions

For centuries we have been stuffing our emotions, pushing ourselves further away from who we are and creating sickness in our lives of perpetual grief and mourning. When an emotion surfaces we have a choice to turn up the volume and listen or to turn off the signal (our bodies are sending us) and ignore the symptoms we are creating that repress the emotions. Usually when we are feeling numb, it is a indication that we have succeeded in dismissing or repressing our emotions. Facing our emotions is not an easy undertaking. Often, we do everything in our power not to cry or we feel that if we allow ourselves to cry we will never stop. Many of us have the idea that we must be strong for others, but that only adds to our holding on to the sadness that has become our story in our struggle through grief. At the instant our emotions surface and we forbid ourselves to emote, we suppress and lock up those emotions, holding ourselves hostage in a world full of pain and suffering.

When we are triggered with a sensory memory, such as hearing a meaningful song, instantly our cellular memory is ignited and our emotional memory stampedes into the moment. Emotions rush in spontaneously and take us back to a certain place and time in our life remembered. Triggers, in any form, can spark a swarm of emotions that bring us into a tug of war between simply feeling like we feel or taking every bit of strength we have and stuffing our emotions back to some hidden place within us.

Holding on to our emotions translates into a silent stress within our bodies, producing toxins that build up over time, creating Dis-Ease as Louise Hay suggests in her book <u>Heal Your Body</u>. These emotions we refuse to release feed our toxic thoughts. Like a computer virus that penetrates our hard drive, this manipulating and misdirecting poisoned thinking infects our internal wisdom and builds the barriers that prevents the emotions from breaking through.

When we embrace our emotions we are doing it out of love and compassion for ourselves as well as creating the mind, body, spirit connection. The internal conflict between our ego and our heart is what we battle in believing that we are safer by not letting our emotions surface versus breaking through and letting go. It is when we are in the moment, with no attachment to what we 'should' or 'should not' be doing that Spirit (our essence) follows.

Consciously Releasing Our Emotions

Through immense grief it is so challenging for us to find ways to embrace our emotions and allow ourselves to release those emotions that we bottle up inside of us. There are so many fears and uncertainties about letting our emotions out and what might happen if we did. We feel them and at the same time hold them in, perpetuating our anguish. We may not feel as though we ever really release our emotions. However, if we look closer, we realize that we are unconsciously releasing our emotions constantly. When we express emotions with a mean-spirited outburst or express any negative self-berating action, we know that we are filled with residual unhealed and unresolved emotions still clogging us with the pain that we absorbed from the event or impact of tragedy that cast us into our grief.

The truth is that we are always releasing our emotions. Even when we are not cognitively aware of our emotional rooted experiences, we release our pain and ill-ease naturally. This is a fundamental part of being human. Just as the body releases toxins, for example when we sweat, we are unconsciously releasing our emotions and toxic thoughts through our moods, outbursts, crying, laughter and even our sadness.

When we consciously release our emotions we recognize we are not taking backward steps. We understand that we are learning to accept and acknowledge our emotions when they surface and we are actually taking important steps forward. It is in this process that we find the courage not to stuff, dismiss, put behind or superficially get over our pain. In this practice of consciously releasing, we continue to go deeper and deeper into the core of who we are. We accept all parts of who we are and we begin to heal ourselves versus harming ourselves and others through our pain. For many of us we can relate to feeling so much better after a good cry because crying is such a natural and universal way of releasing our emotions. After a full cry our body, mind and spirit feel immensely relieved, sometimes to exhaustion. This may lead us into that nurturing empty space of serenity or the peaceful quieting of the storm. It is in that instantaneous flash of memory that soars through us that we simply allow our memory to flourish and our emotions to be expressed through our hearts. This is emotional release.

At times it may feel as though we do release our emotions, that we are making efforts to move forward and embracing our emotions, only to find them coming right back again over and over throughout our lives. Remember, this is a process, a human experience. Until we accept and free ourselves from the pain and torture we put ourselves through by suppressing and denying our emotions, the roller coaster of clusters and layers will continue to surface in our lives.

For many of us we find it difficult to show our emotions around others because our insecurities or fears would suggest that we are vulnerable. We may feel as though being vulnerable is a sign of weakness, yet we know that it takes a great deal of strength and courage to open up a part of us that is authentic and real. Because of this illusion of being weak we stop ourselves from going to the core of our emotions and who we are and choose to hold back and put on our "I'm OK" mask as quickly as possible. This is an instinctive attribute of avoidance. Ultimately avoidance creates an intolerable anxiety that forms barriers to any hope of healing and moving through grief to reclaiming a life of fullness again.

It is important to note that the idea of releasing our emotions is not a free ticket for cruelty or causing harm to another in the name of clearing our emotions. When we release emotions such as anger, rage, hate, and guilt with the intention of healing ourselves, this is an internal process that brings us a sense of relief. However, when we act out our suppressed emotions of anger, rage, hate and guilt in a way that is violent, hostile, and harmful to others and ourselves this is not emotional release, it is self-destruction and revenge.

As we begin to allow ourselves to open our hearts to letting go and connecting with others through our genuine emotions and how we feel, we begin to lead a more authentic life through understanding, compassion, empathy, love, joy, peace and harmony.

Physical Symptoms We May Experience

Tightness in Chest	Fatigue	Breathlessness
Irregular Heartbeat	Headaches	Tremors-Shaking
Change in Appetite	Dry Mouth	Insomnia
Vulnerability to Illness	Nausea	Irregular Bowels
Muscle-ache	Chills	Heavy Perspiration

Mental Symptoms We May Experience

Loss of Control	Confusion	Restlessness
Preoccupation	Fear	Panic Attacks
Social Withdrawal	Anxiety	Flashbacks
Depression	Denial	Suicidal Thoughts
Absent-mindedness	Addiction	Remorse

Emotional Symptoms We May Experience

Sadness	Despair	Helplessness
Anger	Yearning	Nightmares
Abandonment	Crying	Hopelessness
Loneliness	Screaming	Heartache
Blame	Rage	Overwhelm

I'm sitting on the beach in Kauai with
three crosses in front of me. The sound of
the ocean moving in and out and the waves crashing
down onto the shore is surreal.
There are no coincidences in life.

Part Six

A Grieving World

The Anguish of the World

From the heart wrenching brutality and death from wars that plague our planet, the little child killed in a car accident on a remote rural road, to the racial prejudice that poisons are hearts, grief touches all of us. The effects of grief are everywhere, knotted up in the perpetual expression of generations struggling with and passing on the inherited agony of grief's clusters and layers. Individually and collectively we are co-creating and spreading the fear of experiencing our grief and the emotions of loss that come with it.

Our world is one enormous ball of grief and a closer look reveals our global community suffering with an explosion of widespread loss in a commonly shared way. When we step back and look at all of the conflicts, atrocities, violence, destruction, catastrophes and personal tragedies in nations near and far, we see in every aspect of these painful demonstrations that grief is clearly at the root of every clash and discord. This anguish of the world unveils the reality that grief is a universal emotion that transcends every difference between us: age, gender, ethnicity, culture, belief, non-belief, religion, tradition, values, wealth or poverty.

As individuals when we personalize the feeling of the anguish of grief, we personify our isolation and separation. It is in the realization that our pain and sadness of loss is an experience that is being felt by millions if not billions of people and it is this collective that shapes the magnitude of the anguish of the world. Imagine a parent who has been told that their child has died or been killed. Envision millions of people collectively and unconsciously feeling the emotions of loss and sharing a knowingness that goes beyond words in a global community of grief. This invisible kinship is the true essence of the healing potential for the anguish of the world. It is in this kinship that we realize our connection to humanity and understand that no matter how tragic the world looks or how intense the pain in our hearts is, we are never alone in our grief because it is the world that is grieving.

The Torment of Our Actions

Our individual part in the anguish of the world is equal to how we experience grief. The way we communicate and express ourselves in grief, verbally or non-verbally, in our daily life not only affects ourselves and those around us, it also attaches us to a world of pain and sorrow. When we act out upon ourselves or toward others with hate, anger, rage or guilt we ignite further suffering in the world. These are all fear based emotions that can be found in grief that keep us locked in our own pain and anxiety.

When we continue the cycle of self sabotage, self punishment or self destruction in our own lives, we spread emotional devastation, as if it were a plague throughout our world. However, although the outreaching affects of the torment of our actions have an intangible connection, globally we must remember that manifesting these emotions and struggles are inescapable in grief. Having these emotions and releasing them is one of the most important parts in the grieving process.

Even though our actions can create torment in our lives and enable others to do the same, through the healing of our grief we can change our actions and create peace in our lives and those around us. Each of us has a choice to go through our life carrying our own pain and suffering or to take the opportunity to open our minds and hearts to greater possibilities for healing.

Our Secret World of Grief

Each of us has a perception of ourselves no one else sees. Whether we see ourselves as peaceful warriors or being lost in the dark night of our soul is up to us. This is a choice and every choice begins with a thought. In grief most of us feel as if our lives have been ruined, certainly changed forever. The turmoil, chaos and anguish we feel is a part of each one of us. As we realize that our suffering begins in our own minds we find our way to a new understanding that, with every thought, we choose the circumstances we live in. This can be a difficult idea for many of us at first.

Within the heartache of grief, each of us, through our own agony, initiates in our thoughts the idea of an endless life of sadness or not. However, whatever we are feeling, we are not in a wrong place to be in our emotions. It is a natural part of experiencing our grief that there will be times when we feel all is lost as there will be times when we feel the strength to move forward. It is with this swinging of our thoughts that we create the outward appearance of handling life, when inside the emptiness is unbearable. We appear to others to be fine when inside we are really living silently in our secret world of grief.

The painful and complex spiraling of the journey through the clusters and layers of grief has the potential of perpetuating thoughts of emptiness and separation. This state of being strengthens our false image and commits us to living two lives; the life of seeming to be ok and the life of heartache. There comes a time when we acknowledge our thoughts and allow our emotional bodies to feel the sadness and be inspired by our own strengths and willingness to move forward and begin to heal our thoughts and open our hearts to love and compassion for ourselves.

Healing Our Thoughts

If it is only a thought away that keeps us separate from connecting with others, our loved ones and ourselves, what is it that keeps us from changing our thought? Change can be one of the most difficult things in life for people to do; we must first believe that we deserve the change and that it is time to heal.

For years philosophers, scientists and psychologists have studied the mind and discovered how our thoughts can change our life. Some have estimated that we have over 60,000 thoughts a day and for many of us that means we walk through our day basically unaware of all the thoughts we are actually having. And for most of us, we don't realize the unconscious thoughts going through our minds have an action associated with that exact thought.

We may find ways to change our thoughts or reframe our thoughts. The question is, are we healing ourselves through our own reprogramming? Especially in grief, our minds can be like sponges soaking up recycled thoughts from our pain that keeps us stuck in the war zone of despair. A war of hate, guilt, fear and judgment. For the majority of us, we are living in an unconscious world of emotional uncertainty. When we disconnect ourselves through shutting down our emotions, we unintentionally contribute to a world that is broken apart and separate. When we grieve with compassion for ourselves with the purpose of embracing our own healing, we not only heal ourselves, we contribute our part in slowly beginning to heal the world.

There comes a time when each one of us takes responsibility for how we care for ourselves in the healing process. It all begins with us as an individual. The biggest part of healing our thoughts is when there is no thought; no sadness, no pain, no tears, no laughter and no anchor of certainty. There is only a shadowy sense of pure emptiness. This is the space that we feel as though everything is surreal, there is a stillness and peacefulness inside of us without a real single focused thought. We have an unexplainable knowingness that somehow we are going to make it through this fog and there is a sense of finding and connecting with a bigger part of us that feels true and more like the real us.

The Perfect Time and Place

Although it seems impossible and unimaginable, we are all in the perfect place at the perfect time in our lives. No matter where we are in our lives or who has come and gone throughout our life, we are precisely in the place we need to be. In the depths of grief we may feel as though things are far from having happened with perfect timing. For so many, the maze through grief seems brutal, unjust and unfair. It can feel as if we are tied and tangled in our painful emotions in the muddy waters of confusion.

Yet, for so many there does come a time when we feel there has to be a bigger picture to all of this, that there has to be something that makes sense again. When we are in the depths of despair, the universe has a way of bringing forth the signs that are right in front of us.

Sometimes the pieces to the puzzle may come to us in deeply personal ways or signs. The perfect song comes on the radio; we see a rainbow, a shooting star, or a humming bird at a meaningful moment in our day. Maybe we find a better job, make a move, find the strength to help others or as simple as someone asking us for forgiveness.

When we believe, trust and have faith in those moments, we find hope or peace in the serenity of how precious life is and we may begin to recover the meaning of our own purpose. As we fill our hearts with life again, we unwrap the underlying messages of why we are in this place that we find ourselves in and we begin to embrace the spirit of who we are and our part in the world of grief. We realize that when we are connected to our spirit we are in perfect harmony with the universe.

I awoke this morning feeling a little more
hopeful. My body aches, almost as though
others sadness and pain are in my body.
Not sure what part of me is still resisting
stepping into my true self.

Part Seven

Tomorrow

A New Day

There comes a wondrous time when we realize that we are putting one foot in front of the other, leaving the past behind and taking fresh steps into this adventurous journey we call life. The earth beneath our feet feels different; as though we are walking on sacred ground, finding our way through the shadows of the forest and into the rainbow of light. For so many of us this is a day we thought would never come. This new beginning can be scary, yet exhilarating, as we find ourselves making friends with renewal and searching for a new meaning in life.

As day turns into night and night escorts in another day, we now anticipate tomorrow with a belief that there really is a reason to be grateful that we are alive. With the hope of tomorrow, we experience a new day filled with opportunities to connect with others more meaningfully, dissolve into our peaceful inner stillness and realize how precious our life really is. Our eyes are open to brighter possibilities and we know, however the day starts or ends, each moment has its own perfect timing that takes us into the discovery of who we really are. For the first time in what seemed like an endless haze of yesterday's sorrows we can breathe again. We wake up in the now and know the day on the calendar is the day we are living.

Living in the new day we look forward to getting out of bed, being with friends, exercising, ending our addiction, maintaining our recovery, redecorating, eating healthy foods, being intimate, laughing and celebrating holidays. Something is different. The knots of the past have frayed apart and we are free from the limitations that once held us back. There is an appreciation for what was overlooked before. We recognize a change in what we value and what we hold as important to us. This is a time of complete self acceptance. An acceptance of the good, bad, beautiful, sad, cheerful, heartbreaking and heartwarming parts of us coming together as one. We break down the barricade that has kept us separate from ourselves and others and we give ourselves permission to trust life again. In this new vision we take the opportunity to visualize and imagine a new life filled with revitalization, contentment and most significantly, joy. There is no more suffering in silence, holding on to our emotions or keeping ourselves locked in the prison of 'if-only'. These are days filled with the freedom to surrender, positive healing thoughts and the strength to risk life again.

Every moment of the new day opens the door to a new you.

A New You

There will come a day when the storm is far behind us and we realize we have the ability to begin again, like a caterpillar working our way out of our cocoon; we embrace our transformation, ready to soar butterfly free. This realization may be found through the underlying messages that have been there all along, that until now were hidden or pushed away. We move into the unknown; innocent, open and vulnerable with a new trust in ourselves. The smallest things suddenly become a quest for new purpose and inspiration. This is a time beyond grief, surrendering with liberating aliveness in gratitude for whatever life brings, without expectations, demands or conditions. We feel sensations and have experiences that are magical or mystical happening in our lives. We feel a new confidence in how we communicate to our loved ones with a relationship that goes far deeper than words alone. We have a new found security in our life and a desire grounded in a willingness and faith inside us that allows the echoes of our pain, sorrow or difficulty to just be and fade away. We accept it for what it is and do not let it stop us in our commitment to move forward.

A big part of our new passion of acceptance is having a renewed perspective in knowing that the less positive qualities we experience in life are threads in the layers and clusters of grief. As those once devastating and now less harmful traits resurface, we notice our different point of view in how we see them, work through them and eventually move beyond as they pass and disappear from our lives. On the other side of bereavement we touch the breath of who we really are in our greatest potential. We realize the person we once were no longer exists and we reach out to adopt and nurture a new self. With this bigger outlook of life we realize how we are attracted to the positive qualities of our life and how much easier it is to share that part of us with everyone. Even those hearts that were once broken are slowly healing in the glow of a bright light that is in every one of us. Unless we have stopped listening to our hearts all together, we understand something else is steering us.

For many this can be a time of spiritual awakening. No matter what brings us to this place, it is a place where we feel as though we are home. A place where we know and we believe that anything is possible. When we remember or dream of our lost loved ones being with us, our minds melt into an unconscious world where heaven and earth meet, where we realize that the people who touched our lives so meaningfully are with us forever. Although they are with us from another dimension, another world, it is the heart that transcends this world and connects us with them.

Even though there may still be those unexpected gloomy days when all we are hoping for is a better tomorrow, we remember to anticipate the positive potential in everything, as we step our way back into the world and make the world a better place because we are in it.

A New World

The foundation to living in a world understanding grief means living in a world where we are able to identify, with each conscious step we take, our life moving closer to a oneness with the past, present and the future.

In a new world, people are in touch with themselves, their communities and the humanity of our entire planet. Our insight reveals, with each thought – individually and collectively, that there is a Sacred Space that lives in all our hearts with love, compassion and empathy patiently waiting to be tapped into. We have an awareness of our vulnerabilities to self-destruct through unnecessary self-torture and we resist the temptation to fall back into the darkness of our grief or be triggered to release our pain with vengeance.

Because of our own passage through the frontier of loss we embrace our intent to be self-caring and care for others. This is a place where healing ourselves comes first. We understand that love and compassion is the prescription for healing the wounds of grief that live beneath the scars on our hearts and our painful memories; and we comprehend bringing love and forgiveness into our lives as a daily practice not only changes us, it changes the world forever.

Each of us has our own unique gifts to give. The discovery of our personal offerings rarely appears gift wrapped with ribbons and bows. So often, realizing our own meaning in life or finding a greater purpose comes to us through tragedy in the process of life. When we are willing to open these gifts that live within us, we see how rare and special we are and we are also able to see the extraordinary gifts of others. With faith and sureness of the joy our gifts bring, we continue to heal and share the brighter side of our self with the world. We recognize that when we give up on ourselves we give up on something bigger than ourselves; we give up on the world and the opportunities we have to connect with and support one another as we face the unstoppable tides of the tragedies of life that are part of the human experience.

In a new world people in every land and every culture are willing to reach out across our differences and live in harmony; intuitively listening to their inner voice spreading love and compassion through the shared experience and knowingness that all of our pain and fear comes from the single core of our collective grief. And in this knowing we have a perspective never seen before, an unspoken empathy we never knew possible. When the all-encompassing global humanity of grief has been acknowledged and our common ground made visible, people listen with the goodness of their hearts and we realize we don't need to run or hide from the vacuum of grief – for the vacuum is the emptiness that brings us to the threshold of our own healing.

Although grief is a human frailty that is embedded within the template of our existence, we now have an understanding that through thousands of years of evolving beyond superstitions and into self-awareness, the deeper meaningfulness and experience of grief is essential in our ability to transform our lives and heal ourselves from the inside out.

We can no longer deny that grief makes no distinction between gender, race, culture, tradition, religion, ideology or class. This emotional phenomena transcends all man made illusions of separation and division. Because loss and death are a never-ending part of life, we can not pretend that grief will disappear some day from our lives. Yet, how we grieve and the paradigm of mourning will continue to change as we continue to change and realize our humanitarian spirit is linked through our inherited world-wide kinship.

In a new world rooted in compassion and empathy, we see our heartache in the eyes of others who also have been torn apart from the thunder of loss. We begin to recognize that without loss we would have never known grief and to have never known grief is to live in a world without love and kindheartedness for the suffering. It is through this goodwill that a heart to heart connection is made with those dear to us and even the stranger whose eyes silently reveal their grief. We know there is one thing that unites us all, one thing that goes beyond all superficial separation and differences between us. We know that somewhere deep inside each one of us there is something we all share equally. We know Grief Is Our Universal Emotion of Loss.

Made in the USA
San Bernardino, CA
13 January 2013